The Sacred Language of Flowers

Nicole Summers

<u>Disclaimer</u>

The content of this book is for informative purposes only.

The medical benefits of this plants is not intended to be a substitute for medical treatment.

Before using or ingesting any herb or plant for medicinal purposes, consult a physician or a medical herbalist for advice, particularly if you have a known medical condition or if you are pregnant or nursing

Flowers and leaves must be especially cultivated as food grade to be ingested or to be used as tea.

Do not us plants from your florists or local supermarkets as they are not grown for ingestion, they are grown only for decoration and can be full of pesticides and chemicals

This book as well as the poems is copyrighted

Copyright © 2023

The complete book
about birth months flowers

January
Carnation

February
Iris

March
Daffodil

April
Daisy

May
Lily of the Valley.

June
Rose

July
Larkspur

August
Gladiolus

September
Aster

October
Marigold

November
Chrysanthemum

December
Poinsettia &
Holly

Floral Floriography

Each month of the year is represented by a special flower known as "Birth flowers".

Similar too birth stones the flowers are associated with characteristics and qualities that reflect the person which is born in that month.

This book explore this flower, the native country, botanical name, what the flower is associated with, the spiritual meaning and the myth surrounding it. Medicinal and psychological qualities is explored. as well as combinations of flower arrangements to compliment the flowers for various occasions.

This book also aid as a botanical encyclopedia for the florist, the gardener, the romantic at heart, the bride-to-be, great on your coffee table or for your green-thumbed friend.

You will be informed you of the meanings behind the specific flowers and will start to look at flowers with new and refreshed eyes!

Who could say that most flowers have a history in Greek and Norse Mythology?

<u>*My Favourite Flower*</u>

"A Carnation is a
beautiful flower.
Not as elegant as the rose
but rather plain, simple
and versatile.
with a delicate smell
of spices, the wind
and the rain"

January

Carnation

Carnation

Botanical Name:
Dianthus Caryophyllus

Native to:
Native to Italy, Greece, Spain, and Mediterranean countries.

Associated with:
A mothers love

Spiritual meaning:
Devotion and Love

Myth of the Carnation:
First mentioned in the Greek literature. As the legend goes, carnations appeared after the Crucifixion of Christ, growing where the mother of Jesus, the Virgin Mary's tears fell to the earth.

Medicinal Qualities:
The Carnation, renowned for its calming properties on the nervous system, provides respite from muscle tension, inflammation, and swelling. It's essential oil functions as a natural antidepressant, effectively alleviating anxiety and stabilizing moods.

How to use:
Add the whole flower or sprinkle the fresh petals over salad or cooked dishes. Use a few drops of aromatherapy oil in the bath, in a carrier oil or hand and body cream.

Blend well with
Primarily employed as focal flowers, Carnations can also serve as excellent support flowers to enhance other floral arrangements. They pair exceptionally well with bold blossoms such as sunflowers, lilies, or large-headed roses.

<u>Iris Eyes</u>

What is the hue of her eyes?
Blue or purple, sun or cloud?
Once she was so cute and small
yet today all grown up and wise

Can't hold her, Can't hug her,
follow her own way.

All I can do my dear
blue and purple flower...
Is to stay on my knees and pray

February

Iris

Iris

Botanical Name:
Iris

Native to:
Native to Europe and Asia

Associated with:
Royalty

Spiritual meaning:
Wisdom, hope, trust and courage

Myth of the Iris:
In Greek "Iris" translate to "rainbow" and represents the goddess of the rainbow, a messenger for Zeus the Greek mythological god which control the weather, wind, rain and thunder.

Medicinal Qualities:
To treat inflammation, bacterial and viral infections.

How to use:
Do not indigest any form of the plant as it is poisonous. Use aromatherapy oil according to product instructions.

Blend well with
Combine with colours such as deeper plums, red-browns, yellow-greens, grapes and grey. Blend with flowers such as lilies, roses and magnolia leaves.

For a romantic idea take Iris, lavender, dark red small roses, and wrap with purple tissue paper and a dark red ribbon.

<u>Flowers is...</u>

Flowers are sunshine,
Flowers are rain,
Flowers are for happiness and
Flowers are for pain

They are medicine to the body
And food for the soul

"Sunshine provides the human body with Vitamin D, which is essential for physical health and offers mood-boosting benefits."

March

Daffodil

Daffodil

Botanical Name:
Amaryllidaceae Narcissus

Native to:
Native to northern Europe

Associated with:
Spring, beginnings and resilience.

Spiritual meaning:
Seen mostly in easter drawings and bouquets, associated with rebirth and new beginnings.

Myth of the Daffodil:
Associated with Narcissus, son of the Greek god of the river, Cephissus. The son, known for his beauty, fell in love with his own reflection at the pond and the nodding head of the daffodil symbolise him staring at his reflection in the water.

Medicinal Qualities:
Extractions are made out of the daffodil plant to treat Malaria, Inflammatory diseases, Alzheimer's and viral infections. Take only under medical supervision as the Plant is toxic. Oil, can be used in bath water and in carrier oils for stress relief, uplifts the mood and to enhance energy.

How to use:
Use only as an aromatherapy oil according to product
 instructions.

Blend well with
Presents lovely with Tulips, Iris and Gypsophila known as Baby's Breath.

<u>*Where I will be.*</u>

*"They say I'll be pushing daisies
one day, But, my child, that
won't be my way.*

*I'll journey far and wide, Paint
the moon in shades of red, Turn
the sun to purest white, And the
sky, a vibrant green spread.*

*For in the realm of art, you see,
That's where I'll eternally be."*

April

Daisy

Daisy

Botanical Name:
Bellis perennis

Native to:
Native to Europe and areas of mild temperatures in Asia

Associated with:
Love, hope, happiness, beauty, innocence and fun

Spiritual meaning:
Eternal life and faith

Myth of the Daisy
According to Norse Mythology, this was a special sacred flower to Aphrodite who was the goddess of Fertility, love and beauty.

Medicinal Qualities:
Wild daisy tea is normally taken for coughs, bronchitis and inflammation. Aromatherapy oils for relieving of muscle sprains, strains, spasms, arthritis and nerve pain.

How to use:
Add the daisy leaves or buds to soup, sandwiches, salads and use the flower heads as eatable salad decoration. Add essential oils to bath or body creams.

Blend well with
Daisy is a versatile flower to blend, depending on the occasion, it can also be used on its own.

For a lovely bridal bouquet, use with Iris, Gypsophila (Baby's Breath), and rose buds and tie up with a white or gold ribbon.

<u>*Fragile heart*</u>

Delicate little flowers,
Where fairies wander so free,
Resemble little white bells,
Quivering in the soft breeze,
My fragile heart,
You've cast back to me..."

<u>May</u>

Lilly of the Valley

Lilly of the Valley

Botanical Name:
Convallaria Majalis

Native to:
Native to Europe and Asia

Associated with:
Motherhood as well as celibacy

Spiritual meaning:
Purity

Myth of the Lilly of the Valley
According to Norse Germanic mythology, the Daisy
is associates with Ostara who is the goddess of fertility
and purity.

Medicinal Qualities:
Versatile as an aromatherapy oil for conditions such as
urinatory track infections, heart problems, eye infections and
for detoxification, to heal wounds, reduce fever and boost
brain function.

How to use:
Do not eat this plant it is poisonous. Use as an essential or
aromatherapy oil as directed by the manufacturer.

Blend well with
Always lovely together with all types of roses or rose buds.

<u>***More than just Roses***</u>

Roses is for romance
Roses is for Love
They ignite the fire,
Have thorns and give pain
They bloom in the sun
and withstand the rain

Roses capture memories,
yet they cast a spell
Many years later
Their fragrance can tell
if you were in heaven
Or maybe in hell

Capture an eternity
Deep in the heart
Forever and a day
Together
Or
Apart

Rose

Rose

Botanical Name:
Rosa rubiginosa

Native to:
 Asia, North America, Europe and northwest Africa

Associated with:
Love, passion, friendship and joy

Spiritual meaning:
Purity, holiness, sacrifice, wisdom, gratitude and piece.

Myth of the Rose
In Roman Mythology the goddess of flowers "Flora", walked and found her dearest nymph diseased saddened by this she turned him into a pink rose. Bacchus provide scent, Venus add beauty and Mars who is the god of war, gave the rose thorns to protect the roses beauty.

Medicinal Qualities:
Roses is good for stress relieve, anxiety relief and general relaxation. relaxation.

How to use:
All roses are edible and can be used in a variety of foods and as edible food or cake decorations.   Aromatherapy oils to be add to bath water, body lotions and oils.

Blend well with
Blends well with flowers which hides the stem of the rose such as lavender or catmint (Nepeta). Roses with a bit of greens and a ribbon is also a great choice for a bouquet.

<u>Stand tall</u>

"Crumbles from the blue-sky
Fell and splashed on the ground
The Elf's and Nymphs took a brush
and blend it with the grass

Larkspur flower stand tall
Against the wind and rain,
Keep your back to the wall,
In life's relentless strain
Aways protect your heart
Against heartache , betray and pain"

Larkspur

Larkspur

Botanical Name:
Delphinium

Native to:
Central and eastern USA

Associated with:
Dignity, Grace and Strong bonds of love

Spiritual meaning:
Purity

Myth of the Larkspur
Believes from an American Pawnee tribe states that crumbs from the blue sky fell onto the ground and became these beautiful flowers.

Medicinal Qualities:
As an aromatherapy oil, this plant helps with poor memory and attention span.

How to use:
Do not eat this plant it is extremely poisonous.
Use as an aromatherapy oil as directed by the manufacturer.

Blend well with
Blend well with blooms of white, dark blue, lavender, pink, lilac and carmine rose shades.

Lovely bouquets with Gypsophila, roses and pale pink daisies.

<u>Moving on</u>

With dignity and pride
She keeps her head up high
All dressed up and tall
Grow against a wall
A beautiful, sword like flower
Full of beauty, wisdom and power
With dignity and grace
Moved on to the next phase

August

Gladiolus

Gladiolus
(Sword Lily)

Botanical Name:
Gladiolus palustris

Native to:
South Africa

Associated with:
Strength, victory and pride. Resilience not to give up.

Spiritual meaning:
Faithfulness and remembrance.

Myth of the Gladiolus:
Through Greek mythology, links exist between this flower and the Greek god Apollo who accidently killed a beautiful prince with his discus. A Gladiolus flower sprouted after from the body of the prince.

Medicinal Qualities:
Often used in African traditional medicine for constipation, colds and to improve energy levels and general mood.

How to use:
Use the flower without the anthers (part where pollen is produced), in sweet and savoury dishes. Petals can brighten up salads. Aromatherapy oil is also available to add to your bath or in oils or body creams.

Blend well with
Blends well with Lilies

<u>My sister</u>

How would I describe my sister as a flower,
in a garden blessed by nature's grace?
With petals soft, in hues of purple and blue,
her strength and resilience always shine through.
Through life's storms, she stands tall and strong,
an unwavering symbol like a uncomposed song.

Like the aster's starry clusters that gleam,
her wisdom sparkles, guiding like a dream.
With tender care, she guides and supports,
a beacon of light when life distorts.
Together we've grown, side by side,
through laughter and tears, our hearts are tied.

You, my sister, a precious cornflower,
Together or miles apart, our bond unbreakable,
Like a timeless treasure, that only we could find.

September

Aster

Aster

Botanical Name:
Aster puniceus

Native to:
North America, Southern Europe

Associated with:
Courage, Faith and wisdom. Derived from Greek, "Aster" means "Star"

Spiritual meaning:
Faith.

Myth of the Aster:
Through Greek mythology, the Greek god Apollo accidently killed a beautiful prince (who was also his lover) named Hyacinthus, with his discus. Apollo turned the soul of the prince then into a hyacinth flowers so that he could live on after death.

Medicinal Qualities:
Often used in traditional medicines for headache, colds, flu, and as a poultices for healing of wounds. Also beneficial as an aromatherapy oil with antibacterial and anti-viral properties.

How to use:
The leaves and the flower are eatable. Use in sweet and savoury dishes as well as to brighten up salads. The roots can be used in soups and the leaves can be lightly cooked to be used as greens. The Aster can be dried, and hot tea can be made which is beneficial to respiratory conditions. A poultices can be made of the roots and plant and apply to the body for healing wounds.

Blend well with
Asters is a good filler plant with their colours and multi-branched flowering stems.   Asters can be dried and retain their colour. Asters go well with daisies and small roses or rose buds.

<u>Surrealism</u>

Marigold and sunlight
playing in your hair
Little gold sparkles everywhere
Do you believe in magic
Are fairies real?
Was it just a summers dream
Or Is life just surreal?

October

Marigold

Marigold

<u>Botanical Name:</u>
Tagetes Erecta

<u>Native to:</u>
Guatemala and Mexico

<u>Associated with:</u>
Warmth, affection, sun and positive energy

<u>Spiritual meaning:</u>
Mysticism, spiritual connection between life and death.
During the Victorian era, Marigolds was associated with grief and mourning.

<u>Myth of the Marigold:</u>
According to Greek Mythology, Marigold was the daughter of Midas who was the mythical king of Phrygia (known as Asian Turkey). His power was to turn anything into gold and so he did with his daughter. Therefore, the saying "the Midas touch".

<u>Medicinal Qualities:</u>
The flower petals has been used to heal skin conditions of all kinds, bruises, varicose veins and inflammation.
As an aromatherapy oil, Marigold oil can be used to relieve cough, diarrhoea and cramps. Not to be confused with Calendula plant, who looks similar but with different qualities.

<u>How to use:</u>
The Marigold petals and leaves is eatable and can be used in various dishes, as a garnish and can also be dried, infused and used for tea. Use Aromatherapy oil according to instructions.

<u>Blend well with</u>
Good to use on its own or to blend well with greens and rose buds. Especially, yellows, orange, peach and creams.

<u>The unseen</u>

In realms unseen,
where spirits collide,
A battle wages,
fierce and vast.

In the depths of souls,
the war is fought,
Between forces of darkness
and Angels of light

Like warriors of old,
the flowers avail,
With messages from
spirit world
shall prevail.

Chrysanthemum

Chrysanthemum

Botanical Name:
Chrysanthemum

Native to:
East Asia

Associated with:
Durability and honesty. Also used as a get-well flower and to offer condolences as well as sorrow.

Spiritual meaning:
Friendship and healing also to bring love and joy into a house. Spiritual warfare and to protect your home against entities. Stop arguments and keep tempers calm.

Myth of the Chrysanths
In Greek Mythology this flower is seen as a protector of evil spirits and the dark world.

Medicinal Qualities:
Headache, dizziness, high blood pressure. As aromatherapy oil, beneficial for stimulating the mind and senses.

How to use:
The flowers are eatable, but this plant is mostly used as a tea. Aromatherapy oils to be add to bath water, body lotions and oils.

Blend well with
Lovely for any type of bouquet or as cut flowers in a vase. This flowers blend perfectly with rose buds and greens.
Add a ribbon and you have the perfect wedding bouquet.

"Christmas blooms with joy, and the flowers whisper the beauty of the season"

December

Poinsettia and Holly

In the dark of the night

"Like a burst of red fire
in a cold winters night
The wind blow softly
and the stars shine bright

When all is in darkness
and the landscapes painted white
Bursts of red flowers
Bring warmth to the night"

December

Poinsettia

Poinsettia

Botanical Name:
Euphorbia pulcherrima

Native to:
Southern Mexico

Associated with:
Since the 16th Century associated with Christmas

Spiritual meaning:
Good luck, abundance and success.

Myth of the Poinsettia:
Named in Mexico the " Flores de Noche Buena" which translate to "Flower of the Holy Night", this plant flower during Winter season with it star like shape and leaves, representing the Star of Bethlehem. Another legend in Mexico states a Pepita, who was a little girl living in a local village in Mexico, took the advice of an Angel and collected weeds from the field to take to church to offer gifts to Jesus, when placed at His feet, this most beautiful flowers with star like red blooms appears out of this weeds.

Medicinal Qualities:
Laxative and pain relieve. Another benefit is that the leaves absorb trace formaldehyde in the air which may be present in the house.

How to use:
Documented as toxic, recent studies show that this plant is not as highly poisonous as documented before, recent studies show benefits of medicinal benefits as well as extractions for tea and laxatives.

Blend well with
Depending on the occasion this flower can be used alone, with holly and ribbons, with coloured rose buds, greens, and even ivy as a table decoration.

<u>*Seasons in life*</u>

"In the middle of the winter
surround by all snow
The joy that winter can bring
and I get to know

That although life has seasons
there is always a glow
Somewhere in the silent night
red berries start to grow"

December

Holly

Holly

Botanical Name:
Ilex aquifolium

Native to:
Europe, United Kingdom, Wester Asia and Northern Africa

Associated with:
First used at Roman feast of Saturnalia, later adapted to Christmas

Spiritual meaning:
Protection, Peace and Goodwill

Myth of Holly:
According to legend, the unique leaves of the holly tree, act as lightning conductors, protecting the tree and nearby objects.

Celtic priests believed the tree protects against evil spirits and bad luck. The believes was that having this leaves inside the house during the dark winter months and to gain the goodwill from fairies, shelter would be provided for them inside the dwelling with this leaves. Therefore, the holly is associated
with Thor who was the god of thunder in Norse Mythology.

Medicinal Qualities:
Traditionally used as a "Ceremonial cleanser" in certain tribes. Also used for rheumatism, cough, fever and digestive disorders.

How to use:
While the berries is toxic for human consumption, the leaves can be dried and brewed into tea. Leaves cannot be consumed in its raw state due to its sharp edges who can damage the mouth and digestive track.

Blend well with
Holly looks beautiful with poinsettia and red and white rose buds.

<u>*Resilience*</u>

When all the growth are leave less
The holly prevails
Like a guarded shield
In a lifeless field

But somewhere,
You get air
You get up
You go on
And before you know it
you will find the sun

And the season will eventually change
The rain will dry
The clouds will fly
And the sun
The magnificent sun
Will shine

<u>*The Sacred language of Flowers*</u>

Flowers speak where words can't.
and so, the secret language of flowers are real.
Flowers represents joy, happiness, romance, passion,
friendship, endings, sorrow and sadness.

Flowers can be extravagant and flamboyant,
flowers can be simple and plain.
A single flower touch your senses,
what it looks like, what it smells like and how it feel.
They look beautiful in sunshine but needs the rain.

Their fragrance can trigger your thoughts
and some people have the ability
to smell floral scents in their memory,
others think they are insane
but deep inside they treasure an echo,
possibly from happiness
or maybe from pain.

A Single flower picked in the field has the ability,
to mean far more than an expensive bouquet.

Whatever the season,
whatever the reason,
When words can't suffice,
the Secret,
almost Sacred
language of flowers are real.

- Colette

Bonus Recipes

Aster Flower Cake

Ingredients

- 2 cups all-purpose flour
- 2 teaspoons baking powder
- 1/2 teaspoon salt
- 1/2 cup unsalted butter, softened
- 1 cup granulated sugar
- 2 large eggs
- 1 teaspoon vanilla extract
- 1 cup milk
- Edible aster flowers
- Edible flower petals
  (optional, for garnish)

Frosting

- 2 cups heavy cream
- 1/4 cup powdered sugar
- 1 teaspoon vanilla extract

1. Preheat your oven to 350°F (175°C).

2. Grease and flour a round cake pan.

3. In a medium-sized bowl, whisk together the flour, baking powder and salt.   Set aside.

1. In a large mixing bowl, cream together the softened butter and granulated sugar until light and fluffy. Add the eggs, one at a time, mixing well after each addition. Stir in the vanilla extract.

2. Gradually add the dry ingredients to the butter mixture, alternating with the milk. Begin and end with the dry ingredients, mixing just until combined.

3. Pour the batter into the prepared cake pan, spreading it evenly. Gently press the edible aster flowers into the batter, spacing them apart. Be sure to remove any hard stems or rough parts of the flowers beforehand.

4. Bake the cake in the preheated oven for approximately 30-35 minutes, or until a toothpick inserted into the centre comes out clean. Remove from the oven and let it cool completely in the pan.

5. While the cake is cooling, prepare the frosting. In a chilled bowl, whip the heavy cream, powdered sugar, and vanilla extract until   stiff peaks form.

6. Once the cake has cooled, carefully remove it from the pan. Frost the cake with the whipped cream frosting, covering the top and sides.

7. For an extra touch, sprinkle edible flower petals on top of the cake as a garnish. These petals can be from the same edible flowers used earlier or any other suitable edible flowers of your choice.

8. Serve the aster flower cake immediately or refrigerate until ready to serve. Enjoy this unique floral delight!

Rose Petal Swiss Roll

<u>Ingredients:</u>
- 4 large eggs
- 1/2 cup granulated sugar
- 1/2 cup all-purpose flour
- 1/4 teaspoon baking powder
- 1/4 teaspoon salt
- 1 teaspoon rose water
- Edible rose petals
- 1 cup heavy cream
- 2 tablespoons powdered sugar
- Additional edible rose petals (for garnish)

<u>Instructions:</u>

1.Preheat your oven to 350°F (175°C). Line a baking sheet with baking paper.

2.Beat the eggs and granulated sugar together until light and fluffy, using an electric mixer. This process will take about 3-4 minutes.

3.In a separate bowl, whisk the flour, baking powder, and salt.

4.Gradually add the dry ingredients to the egg mixture, gently folding them in with a spatula. Be careful not to overmix

5.Stir in the rose water, ensuring even distribution.

6.Pour batter onto prepared baking sheet, create a thin layer.

7.Bake in the preheated oven for approximately 10-12 minutes, or until the cake is lightly golden and springs back when touched.

8.While the cake is baking, prepare a clean kitchen towel by dusting it with powdered sugar.

9.Once the cake is done, remove it from the oven and immediately invert it onto the prepared towel. Gently peel off the parchment paper.

10.Starting from one short end, roll the *cake and towel together* tightly, forming a spiral. Allow to cool in this rolled-up position.

11.While the cake is cooling, prepare the filling. In a chilled bowl, whip the heavy cream and powdered sugar together until stiff peaks form.

12.Once the cake has cooled, carefully unroll it from the towel. Spread the whipped cream evenly over the cake, leaving a small border around the edges.

13.Sprinkle edible rose petals evenly over the cream.

14.Gently roll the cake back up, using the towel to help you maintain its shape.

15.Transfer the rolled cake onto a serving platter. Garnish with additional edible rose petals on top.

Orange, Lavender & Daisy Cake

Ingredients For the Orange Cake

- 2 cups all-purpose flour
- 1 1/2 teaspoons baking powder
- 1/2 teaspoon baking soda
- 1/2 teaspoon salt
- 1 cup granulated sugar
- 1/2 cup unsalted butter, softened
- 2 large eggs
- 1 teaspoon vanilla extract
- 1 cup freshly squeezed orange juice
- Zest of one orange
- Buttercream, Daisies and lavender to garnish

Instructions:

1.Preheat the Oven: Preheat your oven to 350°F (175°C). Grease and flour a round cake pan (8 or 9 inches in diameter).

2.Mix Dry Ingredients: In a bowl, whisk together the flour, baking powder, baking soda, and salt. Set this dry mixture aside.

3.Cream Butter and Sugar: In a separate large mixing bowl, cream together the softened butter and granulated sugar until the mixture is light and fluffy.

4.Add Eggs and Vanilla: Beat in the eggs one at a time, followed by the vanilla extract, until well combined.

5.Combine Wet and Dry Ingredients: Gradually add the dry mixture to the wet mixture, alternating with the freshly squeezed orange juice. Begin and end with the dry ingredients. Mix until just combined, being careful not to overmix. Fold in the orange zest.

6.Bake: Pour the cake batter into the prepared cake pan and smooth the top. Bake in the preheated oven for 25-30 minutes, or until a toothpick inserted into the centre comes out clean.

7.Cool: Allow the cake to cool in the pan for about 10 minutes, then remove it from the pan and let it cool completely on a wire rack.

8.Decoration: Once the cake has cooled, you can decorate it. Place edible daisy flowers on top of the cake and sprinkle culinary lavender buds around the edges or as desired.

9.Serve: Slice and serve your beautiful

cake with daisy and lavender decorations.

Enjoy!

Thank you for your purchase
Please take a moment
and rate this book.

Nicole
Summers